Who Is on the Sofa?

Seed Learning

sofa

table

bed

bookcase

rocking chair

stool

carpet

lamp

Who is on the sofa?

My grandma is on the sofa.

Who is on the bed?

My grandpa is
on the bed.

Who is on the rocking chair?

My mom is on the rocking chair.

Who is on the carpet?

My sister is on the carpet.

Who is on the stool?

My brother is on the stool.

Who is on the bookcase?

My cat is on the bookcase!

Let's learn more about Cambodia.

Amok